CONTENTS

Words that look **bold like this** are in the glossary.

Insects

The bugs in this book are **insects**.

There are more insects in the world than any other creature. They live in many different **habitats**, from hot, dry deserts to underwater!

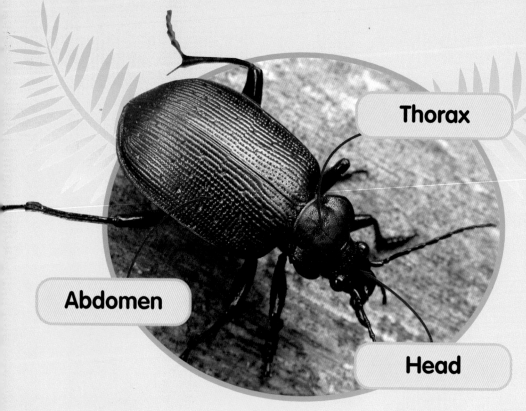

Thorax

Abdomen

Head

There are insects of many different shapes and sizes, but they all have a body made up of three parts.

4

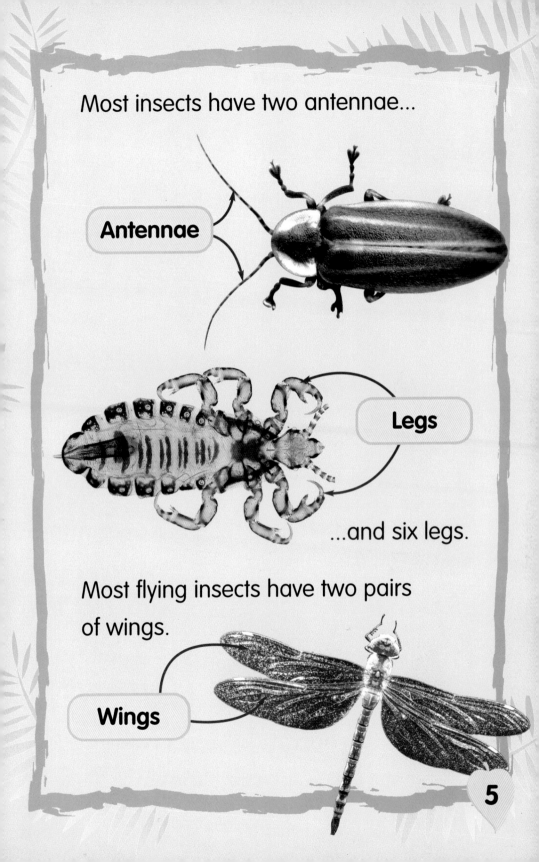

Most insects have two antennae...

Antennae

Legs

...and six legs.

Most flying insects have two pairs of wings.

Wings

5

Ladybirds

There are many different kinds of ladybird, but most are red with black spots.

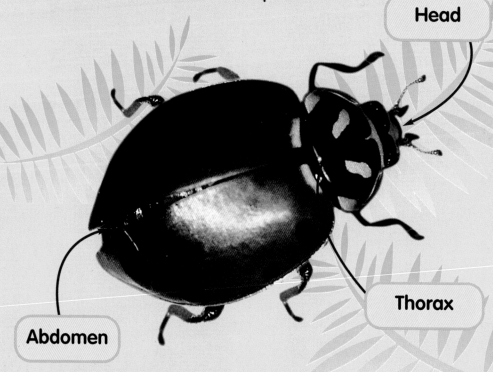

Head

Thorax

Abdomen

There are also yellow ladybirds with black spots and black ones with yellow spots!

6

Their bright colours tell **predators**, such as birds, that they do not taste very nice.

Aphids

Ladybirds live in gardens and parks. They feed on small bugs called aphids.

Ants

Ants live almost everywhere in the world. They live in **colonies** with other ants.

Ants eat other insects. They also eat the **honeydew** made by aphids.

Head

Antennae

Thorax

Ants build large nests with many tunnels.

The nests are often under tree stumps or paving stones.

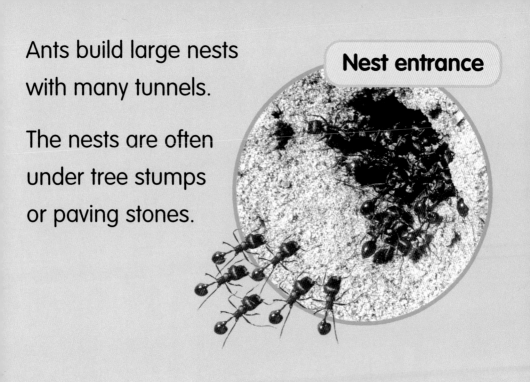

Nest entrance

Abdomen

Dragonflies

The dragonfly is the fastest flying insect in the world.

Wing

Head

Thorax

Abdomen

There are more than 5000 different kinds of dragonfly.

Dragonflies live near ponds, lakes, streams and rivers.

An adult dragonfly has a long body. With its long, thin wings it can hover in the air and dart around.

They feed on flying insects. Sometimes they eat other dragonflies.

Butterflies

There are many different kinds of butterflies.

They have long antennae and their brightly coloured wings are covered with thousands of tiny **scales**.

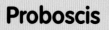
Proboscis

Butterflies have a long tongue like a straw, called a proboscis. They use this proboscis to drink nectar from flowers.

Antennae

Some butterflies live for many years. Others live for about a week and some only live for a day.

x

13

Head lice

Head lice are about the size of a pinhead.

They live on clean hair and feed on human blood.

They have little hooks on the end of their legs.

They hook their short legs around the hair.

Abdomen

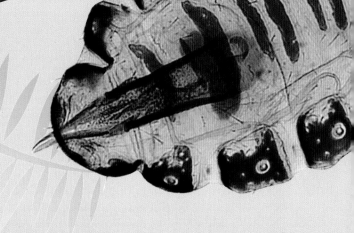

14

Head lice do not have wings so they cannot fly.

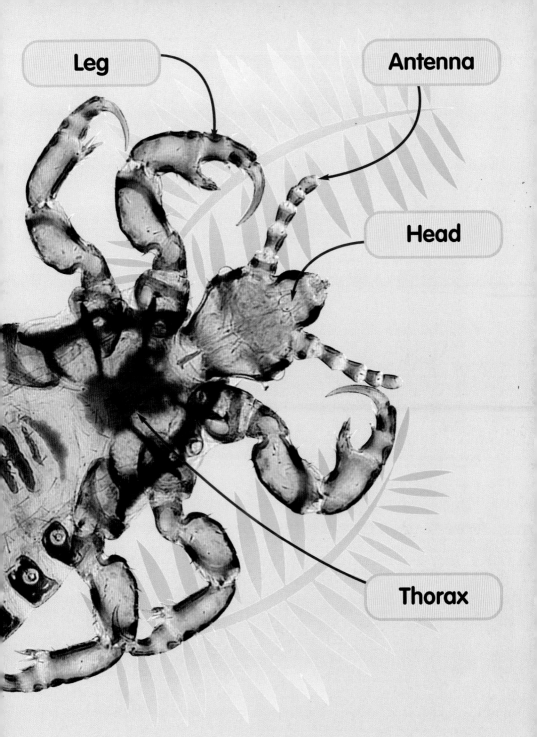

Leg

Antenna

Head

Thorax

They use their legs and hooks to crawl
from head to head.

Aphids

Aphids are tiny insects which live on plants and trees.

They suck **sap** from the leaves and shoots of young plants. This damages the plant and makes it weak.

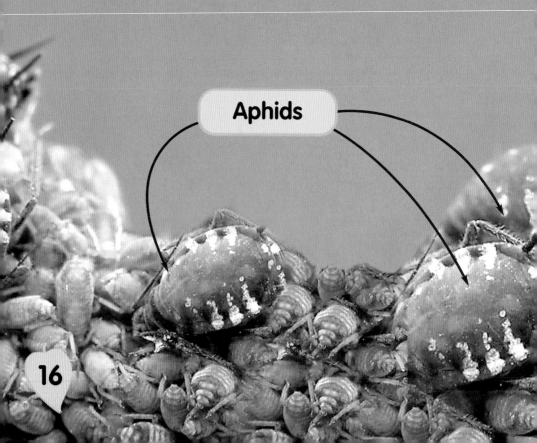

Aphids

Aphids are the main **prey** of ladybirds.

Aphids make honeydew which is eaten by ants.

Ant

Insect life cycles

All insects begin life as eggs laid by an **adult**.

They change as they get older.

Some insects change twice in their lives.
They change from an egg, to a nymph, to an adult.

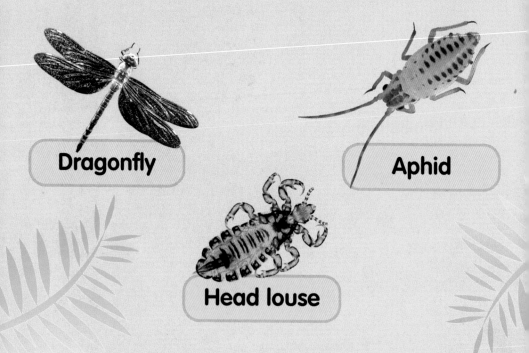

Dragonfly

Aphid

Head louse

An aphid, a head louse and a dragonfly change like this.

Dragonfly life cycle

Eggs

Nymph

Adult

More life cycle changes

Some insects change three times in their lives.

They change from an egg to a larva, then to a pupa and finally to an adult.

They look very different each time they change.

Butterfly

Ladybird

Ant

Ants, ladybirds and butterflies change in this way.

Caterpillar

A butterfly larva is called a caterpillar.

Butterfly life cycle

Eggs

Larva

Pupa

Adult

Thinking and talking about bugs

Where do
dragonflies live?

What changes
take place in the
life cycle of a
ladybird?

How do butterflies
collect nectar from
flowers?

Which insects eat
other insects?

Which insect would you like to be?
Why?

Imagine you are as small as
an ant. Where would you go?

What would you do?

23

adult
Fully grown up.

colonies
Large groups of animals living together.

habitats
The place that is just right for a particular animal or plant in the wild.

honeydew
A sweet liquid made by aphids.

insects
Small animals with bodies that have three parts.

nectar
A sweet liquid in flowers.

predators
Animals that hunt and eat other animals.

prey
An animal that is hunted by another animal for food.

sap
A liquid in plants and trees.

scales
Small, overlapping sections of skin.

shoots
Sections of new growth on plants.

Copyright © **ticktock Entertainment Ltd 2006**
First published in Great Britain in 2006 by **ticktock Media Ltd.,**
Unit 2, Orchard Business Centre, North Farm Road, Tunbridge Wells, Kent TN2 3XF

We would like to thank: Shirley Bickler and Suzanne Baker

ISBN 1 86007 044 2 pbk
Printed in China

Picture credits
t=top, b=bottom, c=centre, l-left, r=right, OFC= outside front cover
Science Photo Library: 7. Shutterstock: 8-9, 10, 16-17, 18-21.
Superstock: 11, 17tr. ticktock photography: 4, 5, 6, 12-13.

I love reading

Bug Watch
by Monica Hughes

Editorial consultant: Mitch Cronick

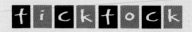